To my mom and dear friends who journey with me - thank you for all your love and support!

To my children who have endured so much - I love you!

WHEN HE'S NOT AN *Ordinary* SINNER

33 DEVOTIONALS FOR THE WOMAN WHO MARRIED A WOLF IN SHEEP'S CLOTHING

JANE POTTER

WHEN HE'S NOT AN ORDINARY SINNER
Copyright © 2025 by Jane Potter

ISBN: 978-1-4866-2604-5
eBook ISBN: 978-1-4866-2605-2

Word Alive Press
119 De Baets Street Winnipeg, MB R2J 3R9
www.wordalivepress.ca

WORD ALIVE
—P R E S S—

Cataloguing in Publication information can be obtained from Library and Archives Canada.

Contents

Introduction

Beloved, I would like to introduce myself. Since I grew up in a Christian home and married a missionary kid, I envisioned a life of ministry and marital bliss.

But I was wrong.

I survived a destructive marriage and am now enduring an expensive and ongoing court battle. It's been a difficult road, but I can attest to God's promises that He is sovereign, faithful, and near to the broken-hearted. It is my hope that my journey can encourage you and validate your experience in some way.

I've chosen to write with a penname: Jane Potter. Jane means "God is gracious." I chose Potter because it pictures our relationship with Jesus: He is the potter, and we are the clay (Isaiah 64:8).

In this devotional, I share passages of scripture, reflections, and healing activities that have helped me, and continue to help me, through my journey. As you read, I pray that you'll find encouragement, peace, and strength from our God.

A note: I am not a counsellor or a doctor, so if you need professional help, please seek it! I'm a sojourner, just like you.

Each devotional has three parts: a scripture reading, a reflection, and an activity.

For the scripture reading, note that I read from many translations because I find they offer different perspectives. Lately I've been enjoying The Passion Translation (TPT), but I will quote from a variety of translations.

The reflection will include my thoughts and likely a personal story, but these personal stories will not include any graphic detail.

The book's activities will be ones I've either discovered on my own, found on the internet, or learned from conferences, counsellors, educators, friends, or mentors. They will include various kinds of journaling, listening to music, and engaging in physical activity and movement. You'll need some supplies: a binder, sheets of medium to heavy plain paper, lined paper, markers, pencil crayons, and a pen.

If you write personal information in your binder, and if there would be a price to pay for these writings—or this devotional book—being discovered, please keep it in a safe place, perhaps even at a friend's house. I've found that there is something special about the brain-to-hand writing process, but if you'd like to type your thoughts you may want to keep it password-protected on your device.

This devotional may be different than others you've read. Many devotionals I've used over the years focus on a wife's need for self-reflection and self-correction in order to improve her marriage. Many women I've met in similar situations naturally self-reflect and try to make corrections, maybe even to a fault.

This devotional, on the other hand, reminds us of our great and mighty God, takes a hard look at a destructive husband's behaviour (whether it's a current, estranged, or ex-husband), and encourages us to walk with integrity despite incredibly hard circumstances. We walk through the fire with Jesus by our side and emerge victorious!

Your experiences are not the same as mine, but our God is the same yesterday, today, and forever. Be encouraged! He is near to the broken-hearted. He is near to you, dear one, and He is near to me. May our good Shepherd restore your soul.

Holy, Holy, Holy

Day and night they never stop
saying: "'Holy, holy, holy is the
Lord God Almighty,' who was,
and is, and is to come."

Revelation 4:8 (NIV)

I want to start this devotional book by worshipping the holy One of Israel. I get discouraged by my circumstances, and honestly the list of heartbreak in my life can seem endless. I'm sure it is for you, too! However, the holiness of our God is greater. Amidst all the difficult and emotionally draining situations, we worship the holy One.

Jesus was crucified, buried, and resurrected for our redemption. He is the pure, spotless Lamb of God who takes away our sin. He is the Lion of Judah! If there is anyone to whom we can entrust our lives, it is Him.

Day and night, the heavenly creatures never stopped worshipping the Lord. He always was, always is, and forever will be. In the middle of our heartache, let us never stop praising the Lord.

ACTIVITY:

My favourite band of my youth was Petra, and I recently had the opportunity to attend a concert of theirs with my teenage daughter. It was a dream come true! I was so excited to share such a powerful concert with her. We loved every minute.

At the concert, lead singer John Schlitt declared that rock is very exciting music and Jesus is the most exciting topic, so it just makes sense to combine them. I couldn't agree more!

If you're not a Christian rock fan, I'm easing you in gently. These songs can be found on YouTube, or any other place you listen to music. If Christian rock absolutely is not your thing, that's perfectly fine. Just choose a song that glorifies God and resonates with your spirit.

I don't know who coined the expression "motion creates emotion," but it was certainly true for me at the Petra concert. I'm sure my emotional reaction was the result of a mix of things: my memories, the message, and the motion!

Here are a couple of Petra songs that proclaim this powerful and exciting message: "Salvation Belongs to Our God" and "Lovely Lord." As you play these songs, worship God with your body. Bow in worship. Stand and wave your arms. Do whatever comes to you. Praise Him.

You can do this activity alone in your room or with your kids, if they're around and need to get their bodies moving, too.

If you're like me, you may have been raised to believe that dancing leads to… well, danger. I didn't realize until later in life that movement has a healing impact on us. Let's worship the King!

Angelic Worship of the Lamb

> Then I looked, and I heard the
> voices of myriads of angels in
> circles around the throne, as
> well as the voices of the living
> creatures and the elders—
> myriads and myriads! And as
> I watched, all of them were
> singing with thunderous voices:
> "Worthy is Christ the Lamb
> who was slaughtered to receive
> great power and might, wealth
> and wisdom, and honor,
> glory, and praise!"
> **REVELATION 5:11–12 (TPT)**

Can you imagine this scene? Can you imagine being swept up in the thunderous chorus of myriads of angels? I'm sure we'd be brought to our knees and flat on our faces in worship. It is truly a celebration of God's glory.

Friends, the Lord our God is worthy! He has all power and might. Think of all the Bible stories in which God has shown His power, as well as all the passages that reference His mighty arm and strong hand.

He is mighty to save! He is worthy to receive wealth. All resources are His! Because He has all wisdom, He is more than capable of handling our problems and bringing about His best in our lives. And He gives wisdom to all who ask Him.

To honour someone is to hold them in high esteem. God deserves the highest honour and these angels, living creatures, and elders certainly acknowledged His place above every other living creature.

Let us praise the One who is above every other name. God is omnipresent, omnipotent, and omniscient. Beloved, this is the God you have in your corner!

ACTIVITY:

Doodling to worship songs in my journal has brought me so much peace over the years. I pick a song that has a particular meaning to me in the moment and doodle words and designs to accompany it.

Journal-doodling may be a good option for you as well. For this passage of scripture, I recommend three songs: "Agnus Dei" by Michael W. Smith, "God All-Powerful" by ARISE Worship, and "Ancient of Days" by, you guessed it, Petra!

Get out your binder, a plain piece of paper, some markers, and pencil crayons, or whatever else you have available. Get comfortable. As you listen to a song, write, draw, and colour along. Let the lyrics and music resonate as you worship the Lord our God. Pause the music when you need to. Or if you need more movement in your life, dance! Whatever you choose to do, worship the King!

God Is Holy and Hates Sin

There are six evils God truly
hates and a seventh that is an
abomination to him: putting
others down while considering
yourself superior, spreading lies
and rumors, spilling the blood
of the innocent, plotting evil
in your heart toward another,
gloating over doing what's
plainly wrong, spouting lies in
false testimony, and stirring up
strife between friends. These
are entirely despicable to God!

PROVERBS 6:16–19 (TPT)

Have you ever heard that God hates divorce? I've heard it a million times.

Before my ex and I were married, he told me that his relatives didn't want him to marry me because my parents were divorced. I would surely file for divorce, because my mother had. He made it clear that if we ever divorced, everyone would believe it was my fault.

I didn't think we would divorce. We were both professing Christians, and I thought that was the only requirement for a healthy marriage. It isn't.

I believe the evils listed in this passage contributed to our divorce. I'm not going to lie: when I initially read Proverbs 6, my ex was the first person to come to mind. The passage describes him to a T![1]

Speaking of spreading lies, it honestly amazes me how the lies can just roll right off his tongue, even with the evidence right in front of his face. He plots evil schemes and finds pleasure in pitting people against each other. And he definitely pits people against me. Truth be told, the only person he cares about is himself.

I take comfort in knowing that God hates my ex's lies, evil schemes, duplicity, and manipulations even more than I do. His actions are an abomination to God!

The verbs in this passage indicate that the action is purposeful and ongoing—putting others down, plotting, gloating, and stirring. We're all capable of these sins.

The question is, if confronted, does this person acknowledge, apologize, and make amends? Or does this person continue sinning even after being confronted?

We may be able to hide our motives from others, or at least cause people to second-guess our motives and give us the benefit of the doubt, but we can't hide it from God, and neither can my ex. God doesn't minimize or justify these actions. He calls them despicable!

ACTIVITY:
How do you feel when you commit one of these sins? Do you feel the nudge of the Holy Spirit? Do you offer an apology and make amends to the person you offended?

---

[1] Except for the part about spilling blood.

I learned a 4-step process at a conference, and it has been helpful. It goes like this:

1. Acknowledge: Name the action.
2. Apologize: Offer an apology for your action and the fallout.
3. Make amends: How will you correct it? Will you pay for something you broke? Will you correct a lie you told?
4. Recommit: How will you commit to doing things differently?

Here's an example. Let's say I borrowed a blouse from a friend, and I stained it. I feel awful and try to get the stain out, but I can't. I take it to the drycleaners, but they can't remove the stain either. Now I feel bad and need to apologize.

1. Acknowledge: "I borrowed your blouse and I stained it."
2 Apologize: "I apologize for my carelessness."
3 Make amends: "I tried to get the stain out, but I couldn't. I took it to the drycleaners, but they couldn't get it out either. I'll buy you another blouse."
4 Recommit: "In the event that I borrow another item from you, I'll take extra precautions to return it in the same condition in which you lent it to me."

Who is someone you need to apologize to? Practise this template.

On a side note: there is no guarantee that your apology will be accepted.

What Does God Value?

There are six evils God truly
hates and a seventh that is an
abomination to him: putting
others down while considering
yourself superior, spreading
lies and rumors, spilling the
blood of the innocent, plotting
evil in your heart toward
another, gloating over doing
what's plainly wrong, spouting
lies in false testimony, and
stirring up strife between
friends. These are entirely
despicable to God!
PROVERBS 6:16–19 (TPT)

Today's passage is the same as yesterday's. The evils that God hates are actions that destroy relationships, reputations, and even lives. It makes sense that God values the opposite of these behaviours.

When I read it and think of the opposite values, I conclude that God values all people, and we should, too. We don't have the right to consider ourselves superior to others and place others beneath us. He also values honesty, especially as it relates to another person's reputation.

This passage tells us not to spread lies for the purpose of ruining another's reputation, but my ex twisted this teaching to silence me. To be clear, we are not instructed to keep quiet and hide sin. While we don't have the freedom to share what has happened with everyone, we don't ruin others' reputations by sharing the truth with authorities, counsellors, mentors, or close friends. We're supposed to expose the ugly deeds of darkness (Ephesians 5:11).

God values life! He values your life and your kids' lives! This reminds me of when the Hebrew midwives disobeyed Pharoah's command to kill the Hebrew boys. The midwives lied to him, and they spared the lives of the innocent (Exodus 1:18).

God also values people and relationships, which means extending good will toward others, living rightly, and giving truthful testimony.

ACTIVITY:
What are your values? On the next page, I've included a list of core values. Circle your top ten, then your top five, and then your top three values.

How do you feel when you live within your top values? I know that I feel great! One of my top values is honesty. When I step out of this, I feel bad and know that I need to make amends.

This exercise, which I learned from counselling, also helped me see my ex's values. I always wondered how he could live with himself—and then I realized that his values are different from mine, and different from the set of values he claims to have. I realized that he only values himself. When I realized that, everything made sense. In his mind, he had nothing to feel bad about because he was living in accordance with his values.

LIST OF VALUES

Achievement	Curiosity	Independence	Recognition
Adventure	Determination	Influence	Reputation
Ambition	Discipline	Intelligence	Respect
Authenticity	Diversity	Justice	Responsibility
Authority	Excellence	Kindness	Security
Autonomy	Fairness	Knowledge	Self-Respect
Balance	Faith	Leadership	Service
Beauty	Fame	Learning	Spirituality
Boldness	Family	Legacy	Stability
Career	Fidelity	Love	Status
Challenge	Financial freedom	Loyalty	Succes
Collaboration	Freedom	Meaningful work	Teamwork
Community	Friendship	Nature	Trustworthiness
Compassion	Fun	Openness	Unity
Competency	Generosity	Optimism	Wealth
Confidence	Growth	Peace	Wisdom
Contentment	Happiness	Pleasure	Others:
Contribution	Health	Poise	_____
Courage	Honesty	Popularity	_____
Creativity	Humour	Productiveness	_____

God Is My Protector

Do not be afraid, for I have
ransomed you. I have called
you by name; you are mine.
When you go through deep
waters, I will be with you.
When you go through rivers of
difficulty, you will not drown.
When you walk through the
fire of oppression, you will not
be burned up; the flames will
not consume you. For I am the
Lord, your God, the Holy One
of Israel, your Savior.

ISAIAH 43:1–3 (NLT)

One morning after our separation, I cried and prayed. This was
the scripture the Lord spoke to me. I was overcome with emotion
and gratitude. The holy One had not forgotten me. In fact, He
loves me and calls me His own!

The Lord told me, "Don't be afraid." I haven't done a word
study on this, but it has to be one of God's most frequently used
statements. He knew what I was going though, as well as what was
still to come. He wanted me to know that I was safe in His arms.

God never promised to remove my problems. In fact, problems are a certainty! The Bible says that *when* I go through the

deep waters, *when* I go through the rivers of difficulty, *when* I go through the fire of oppression, He will be with me. Sometimes it feels like the fires will turn me to ash, but He won't let it happen. He is the Lord my God, the holy One of Israel, and I am His child.

We don't ever know what the next moment brings, but my separation period was so intense that I didn't seem to have any real idea what would happen in the next moment. This is a scary place to be. But God says, "Don't be afraid." Why? Because He is the holy One of Israel!

ACTIVITY:

What are your deep waters, rivers of difficulty, and fires of oppression? What overwhelms you? What are you afraid of?

Let's do a brain dump. Take ten to fifteen minutes to write down any fears that come to mind. Then read your list.

First, circle or highlight the fears you can solve and create a to-do list. Can you make a phone call or write an email you've been putting off? Do you have questions about an upcoming court hearing? If so, is there a lawyer you could talk to? Can you consult with a lawyer for free? Is there a strained relationship that needs attention?

Tackling these tasks is an important part of self-care because it alleviates our worries.

Second, which fears aren't likely to happen? My ex would spout all kinds of lies to paralyze me with fear. He threatened to take the kids, or take one particular child (his favourite) and leave the other (his scapegoat) with me. He would taunt me as we waited in the foyer before entering the courtroom. He would blatantly lie in his affidavits, and I was afraid the judge would believe him. When I told him I was leaving, he challenged me by saying, "With what money?" I was a stay-at-home mom, so the fear was real, but God has provided.

Which fears from the pit of hell can you just cross right off your list?

Third, what are the fears you have no control over? Take the Lord's words to heart. Do not be afraid. Beloved, you are His. He will not let you drown. He will not let you be burned. He is with you!

Do you want a song? Try "Trading My Sorrow" by Darrell Evans, although note that many artists have covered this song.

A Friend Loves at all Times

A dear friend will love you no
matter what, and a family sticks
together through all kinds
of trouble.
PROVERBS 17:17 (TPT)

When I read this proverb, I had many thoughts. After deciding to leave my husband, I had so-called friends drop me like a bag of bricks. I had acquaintances turn around when they saw me coming down the grocery aisle. Two of my brothers wrote letters of support for my ex for use in affidavits. My dad and his wife believe and support my ex, and my dad wrote a letter to me saying that he would welcome me back with open arms once I started handling things in a biblical way. Many family members have chosen not to "take sides."

When it comes to family, my mom is my only solid supporter. Many friends and family members have chosen to be my ex's flying monkeys, cutting ties with me. It's incredibly painful.

Does this mean that the Bible isn't true?

I think of proverbs as nuggets of truth. The purpose is not to catch all the different nuances, though, because then they couldn't be so concise. *The Progress Index* wrote, "Think of Proverbs as a slice of the truth, not the whole truth for every situation."[2]

---

[2] Tom Lovorn, "Book of Proverbs Should Be Understood as Principles for Living, Not Promises for Life," *The Progress Index*. September 10, 2014 (https://www.progress-index.com/story/news/2011/08/06/book-proverbs-should-be-understood/36452367007).

The friends and acquaintances I mentioned aren't dear friends. I certainly do, however, have very dear friends who have journeyed with me through this process.

When my ex and I first separated, he apologized to many people in my life for how he had treated me and our children. Everyone, that is, except me!

I should say that his apologies were nothing like the apology template we discussed previously. His apologies didn't even touch the surface of our issues.[3] He was attempting to demonstrate a contrite spirit.

As I mentioned, some family members believed him. But when he apologized to my close friends, they saw right through him! They said something along the lines of, "Okay, buster. I hope what you're telling me is true, but if not, may God deal with you ever so severely! Leave her alone. You've wreaked enough havoc in her life!"

These dear friends and my mom are the kind of people today's passage speaks of. They love me no matter what, and I love them no matter what. We stick together in all kinds of trouble. We can be vulnerable together, and there is only safety and love between us, never judgment. We believe the best of each other.

ACTIVITY:
I first heard the term "Square Squad" at a conference, but I think Brené Brown coined the term.[4] Your Square Squad loves you no

---

[3] This should have been a huge red flag to my family members, but it wasn't. They bought it and still hold me responsible for our divorce.

[4] "Who's in Your Square Squad?" *Your Time to Grow*. Date of access: April 5, 2024 (https://yourtimetogrow.com/whos-in-your-square-squad).

matter what. They accept you—no, they love you!—warts and all! They give you honest feedback because they want the best for you, and you can receive it even though it stings.

As we know from Proverbs 27:6, *"Faithful are the wounds of a friend [who corrects out of love and concern], but the kisses of an enemy are deceitful [because they serve his hidden agenda]"* (AMP).

There are only four to eight people in this squad. And if your significant other is anything like mine, he's nowhere near this square! His feedback is unreliable at best.

Who's in your Square Squad? Write their names in the box below. Treasure your Square Squad because they're your people. Precious one, you are loved.

MY SQUARE SQUAD

```



```

Thank the Lord for your Square Squad. Treasure them and keep them close.

The Love Chapter

Love is patient and kind. Love
is not jealous or boastful or
proud or rude. It does not
demand its own way. It is not
irritable, and it keeps no record
of being wronged. It does not
rejoice about injustice but
rejoices whenever the truth
wins out. Love never gives
up, never loses faith, is always
hopeful, and endures through
every circumstance.
1 CORINTHIANS 13:4–7 (NLT)

Whenever I've read or studied this passage, it has been in terms of asking the question: does this describe me? It's an important question.

I remember an exercise in Sunday School where we replaced the words "love" and "it" in this passage with our own names, to see if it read accurately. It's important to be self-reflective and walk the path of love, even when it's difficult.

Undoubtedly, love and longsuffering are necessary for lasting relationships. We're even called to love our enemies and pray for our persecutors (Matthew 5:44). The love chapter describes how we can live in community with one another.

But I'm human. Sometimes I'm not patient or kind and I get irritable when I let my frustrations build up or I haven't had enough sleep. Sometimes I get caught up in tit-for-tat. When I behave this way, I take care of myself, get back on track, and try to do things better next time. I want to love my children, family, friends, and others well.

These verses were weaponized by my ex, his flying monkeys, and even church teaching.

I participated in a counselling class at which I had to write down his offences toward me to process my pain. I kept my binder hidden in our closet.

One day when the children and I were visiting my mom, he was at home looking for a piece of clothing when he found my binder. He was livid! He told me repeatedly over the course of several months that love keeps no record of wrongs. He even brought this up in sneaky ways when we were among family or friends. When it fit, he'd quote the phrase during discussions so I would know what he was referring to. The others would nod in agreement, even though they may not have understood the inference. Or maybe they did.

Interestingly, according to him, the problem was my list, not his actions.

In an effort to appeal to my desire to be godly, or perhaps in an effort to make me stay, many people told me that love never gives up on a person or a marriage, never loses faith that God can heal a marriage, never gives up hope that things will get better. And most importantly, love endures through every circumstance, especially a marriage, because every marriage is challenging.

Does this message sit well with you? It does not sit well with me. I find myself thinking, "Yes, but…" For these people, there are no "Yes, buts." There is only "Be more loving and he'll come around." That isn't true. This mindset only breeds entitlement. A marriage in which one person expects to be loved but doesn't extend love is unhealthy and unsustainable.

The truth is that we need to see our situation accurately, and writing helps us face it clearly. The reality for me was that things were bad.

Further, God does not override a person's free will. If a person wants to keep sinning, they can! Our hope is in God, and hope is not foolish when placed in Him, but I realized that I was foolish to expect my circumstances to improve when my then husband was continuing his downward spiral into the deepest, darkest pit. He's still spiralling, and there is no evidence that he wants to climb out.

I first heard the term *hopium* from Patrick Doyle's videos on YouTube. When we take hopium, we are hoping that a relationship will improve without any evidence that it will turn around.

Yes, part of growing is enduring hard things. I feel so brave when I've encountered a difficult situation, handled it (either poorly or effectively), and learned a lesson. I press on and grow.

Staying in a destructive marriage is not that. It's nearly impossible to grow in a destructive marriage because, as in my case, he constantly set me up to fail. He was crushing my soul.

ACTIVITY:

Let's contemplate a different question: do these verses describe the destructive man in your life? This question elicited a dose of reality for me. I replaced the words "love" and "it" with my ex's name.

Note that you may need to brace yourself for this exercise. We don't normally use scripture this way, but it can reveal the truth: the destructive man in your life may not be an ordinary sinner.

The exercise may reveal that he is never patient or kind—and if he is, it's for a purpose. He is often jealous and boastful and proud and rude. He always demands his own way. He is regularly irritable. He keeps records of your wrongs, distorts them, and uses them against you. He rejoices in and is quick to participate in injustices, but he never rejoices when the truth wins out. In fact, he does everything in his power to prevent the truth from coming out. He doesn't persevere or endure through every circumstance.

My ex is the antithesis of love, even though God calls him to live a life of love, too.

A loving wife cannot carry a marriage, but an unloving husband can destroy it. It doesn't take two to destroy a marriage, but it does take two loving people to repair and grow a marriage.

How does your husband fit into this passage? Is he an ordinary sinner who does his best? When he messes up, does he correct himself? Is he open to feedback? Or is he the opposite of this passage, like my ex? Does he take pleasure in causing you pain and trouble?

If he's that guy, I grieve with you. Take time to journal and process this information. If you realize that he's the antithesis of love, don't point it out to him in either anger or love, because that will only make things worse. This exercise lets you know the kind of person you're dealing with.

Evil Desires

Instead it is each person's own
desires and thoughts that drag
them into evil and lure them
away into darkness. Evil desires
give birth to evil actions. And
when sin is fully mature it can
murder you! So my friends,
don't be fooled by your
own desires!

JAMES 1:14–16 (TPT)

I don't know about you, but I believed that I could influence his responses by how I spoke and acted. When he did something to hurt me, I let him know. I thought that if I prayed about what I was going to say and how I was going to say it, he would care and receive it.

I was wrong.

When he looked at porn and I told him how much it hurt me, I thought he would want to stop. I thought he would want to put safeguards on the computer.

I was wrong.

I thought that he would change when things got so bad that I involved the police. He changed for a few weeks, but then he was right back to his old habits. I realized that nothing I said or did influenced him to change for the better, and the truth is that his own evil desires gave birth to his own evil actions.

I also thought that God would change him, and I prayed to this end. I prayed that he would be thoughtful and considerate. I prayed that he would stop using porn. I prayed that he would be the man of God he presented himself to be.

While I was praying one afternoon, God sliced through my prayer to tell me that he was never going to change. At first I didn't believe this was God's voice, because I believed God could change anyone. I believed the Holy Spirit could change him.

As I sit here ten years later, I know that God did indeed speak to me. My ex has never changed for the better. He shows no signs of repentance.

God spoke truth to my heart that day, but it took me several years to believe it. I didn't want to believe it because I wanted my marriage and family to be healthy and godly. I realize now that God doesn't override my ex's evil desires.

Today's passage from James also serves as a caution to me. If I am lured into darkness, it's on me. Before confronting my then husband about his behaviour, I would realize that I could pray and think about my words or I could scream and yell. Neither confrontation changed his behaviour for the better. When he antagonized me and I reacted, and I saw that gleam in his eye, I realized that he was just having fun.

I wasn't having fun. I didn't like flying off the handle or playing into his hand. Not only would I feel embarrassed by my reaction, I would be giving him fodder. If the kids were around, he'd say, "Mommy's having a bad day today."

We all run the risk of giving in to our evil desires, but I wanted to be proud of my conduct.

I've often wondered why he behaved as he did. I would go round and round in circles trying to figure out the why, but it didn't help me. I was still left on the receiving end of his destructive actions. Here is the bottom line: his evil desires caused him to spiral down into the pit of darkness.

ACTIVITY:
For your activity today, I recommend doodle-journaling as you listen to "Build My Life" by Pat Barrett.

God Sustains You

In this passage I have inserted a few of my own responses in square brackets.

Listen to my prayer, O God.
Do not ignore my cry for
help! *[Please don't ignore me!]*
Please listen and answer me
[Please answer me!], for I am
overwhelmed by my troubles.
*[I'm so overwhelmed! Make it
stop!]* My enemies shout at
me, making loud and wicked
threats. They bring trouble on
me and angrily hunt me down.

My heart pounds in my chest.
[What is going to happen next?]
The terror of death assaults me.
Fear and trembling overwhelm
me, and I can't stop shaking.
[Literally. I'm so terrified!] Oh,
that I had wings like a dove;
then I would fly away and rest!
*[This sounds heavenly! When
can I have a reprieve?]* I would
fly far away to the quiet of the

wilderness. How quickly I
would escape—far from this
wild storm of hatred.

Confuse them, Lord, and
frustrate their plans *[Yes,
please!]*, for I see violence
and conflict in the city. *[I
saw violence and conflict in
our own home!]* Its walls are
patrolled day and night against
invaders, but the real danger
is wickedness within the city.
*[Absolutely! Even inside our
own family.]* Everything is
falling apart *[It sure is! What a
mess.]*; threats and cheating are
rampant in the streets.

It is not an enemy who taunts
me—I could bear that. It is
not my foes who so arrogantly
insult me—I could have hidden
from them. *[That's true! I tried
to hide from him, but I could not.]*
Instead, it is you—my equal,
my companion and close friend.
*[I felt the deep pain of betrayal
from my husband.]* What good

fellowship we once enjoyed
as we walked together to the
house of God. *[I thought so, too,
at the beginning.]*

Let death stalk my enemies *[Yes,
please.]*; let the grave swallow
them alive *[That would be great!]*,
for evil makes its home within
them. *[Without a doubt, it does.]*

But I will call on God, and the
Lord will rescue me. *[This is
the truth.]* Morning, noon, and
night I cry out in my distress,
and the Lord hears my voice.
*[This is also the truth. He does
hear me. He hears you.]* He
ransoms me and keeps me safe
from the battle waged against
me, though many still oppose
me. *[Many friends and family
still oppose me.]* God, who has
ruled forever, will hear me and
humble them. *[Yes, He will.]* For
my enemies refuse to change
their ways; they do not fear
God. *[My ex steadfastly refuses.]*

As for my companion, he betrayed his friends; he broke his promises. *[Countless broken promises!]* His words are as smooth as butter, but in his heart is war. *[Don't I know it. He is so divisive.]* His words are as soothing as lotion, but underneath are daggers! *[And I sure felt those sharp, deadly daggers!]*

Give your burdens to the Lord, and he will take care of you. *[This is His promise even when it doesn't feel like it.]* He will not permit the godly to slip and fall. *[Truth!]*

But you, O God, will send the wicked down to the pit of destruction. *[Yay!]* Murderers and liars will die young, but I am trusting you to save me. *[Trusting in God, who is always trustworthy.]*

Psalm 55:1–23 (NLT)

This psalm certainly encouraged me! I can relate to David.

I have wondered whether God was listening. I was tired of being tormented by a person who said he loved me. I was being chastised by family members who said they loved me, but instead they supported him.

I wanted to fly away. I wanted my ex to be destroyed by his lies.

And in the end, I believe that God sustains me.

This psalm is a lament, and a lament has four parts:

1. Turning to God in prayer.
2. Bringing our complaints.
3. Asking boldly.
4. Choosing to trust (or praise). [5]

David turned to God in prayer, begging God to listen to him.

Then David immediately shared his complaints with God. I don't know about you, but I can surely relate to his complaints.

Next he made his bold requests.

And finally he called upon the Lord, believing that God would deal with his enemies and rescue him.

Which parts of this psalm resonate with you? The whole psalm resonates with me, but a few verses particularly catch my eye.

In Psalm 55:6, David expresses his desire to flee. Have you ever wanted to escape?

---

[5] Mark Vroegop, "Lament Leads to Praise," *Mark Vroegop*. Date of access: April 5, 2024 (https://www.markvroegop.com/blog/lament-leads-to-praise).

I learned that doves fly into the wilderness and perch in holes in the rocks to hide from birds of prey.[6] Well, I wanted to run away and hide from the predators, especially the one I married.

One of my pastors told me that my ex was the most dangerous predator of all. "His words are smooth like butter," he said, "but in his heart is war."

At different times in his life, my ex was a missionary, pastor, church board member, evangelist, volunteer, and faithful tither. He was a delightful Christian man when people were around and a wolf in secret.

I often wondered whether he knew his gameplan, but evidently he did. When I told him that I was leaving, he scoffed.

"No one will believe you," he said.

I believed him, and he silenced me for many years.

As Psalm 55:20 states, *"As for my companion, he betrayed his friends; he broke his promises"* (NLT). My ex didn't just ruin his relationship with me; he also ruined friendships and business partnerships because of his lies and broken promises.

This psalm also contains an imprecatory prayer. I had no idea imprecatory prayer had a name! All I knew was that David often appealed to God's justice, and he prayed that God would deal ever so severely with his enemies.

An imprecation is a spoken curse. It's certainly uncomfortable to talk about these "unchristian" feelings. Maybe you don't have these feelings, but I sure did! And King David did, too! An

---

[6] David Guzik, "Psalm 55: Trusting God Against a Treacherous Enemy," *Enduring Word.* Date of access: April 5, 2024 (https://enduringword.com/bible-commentary/psalm-55).

imprecatory prayer is praying that God, in His justice, will harm the offender.

The truth, my friend? This speaks to my soul! A friend introduced me to Jon Uhler, and I learned about imprecatory prayers while poking around his website.[7] I long for justice and desperately want my ex to be held accountable for his actions.

ACTIVITY:

Write your own imprecatory prayer. I know my feelings, thoughts, and concerns have been dismissed over the years, but David never minimized his feelings, and neither does God. We don't need to either. Appeal to God's justice.

1. Address the Lord.
2. Name the injustice.
3. How should the offender be punished?
4. Put your trust in God.

During a time when I was struggling, I called a friend to vent and receive comfort and advice. She sent me the YouTube link of a song her children were singing in church based on Psalm 55:22 called "Cast Your Cares" by Seeds Kids Worship. It was this song that introduced me to the idea in this devotional. The song is catchy! You'll be singing it all day. Don't say I didn't warn you!

---

[7] "Podcasts," *Survivor Support*. Date of access: August 13, 2024 (https://www.survivorsupport.net/podcasts).

Think on These Things

And now, dear brothers and
sisters, one final thing. Fix your
thoughts on what is true, and
honorable, and right, and pure,
and lovely, and admirable.
Think about things that are
excellent and worthy
of praise.
PHILIPPIANS 4:8 (NLT)

What thoughts plague your mind? Many of my thoughts aren't true, honourable, right, pure, lovely, or admirable, let alone excellent and praiseworthy. In fact, many of my thoughts lead me down dismal roads and leave me feeling worried and anxious. Our thoughts lead to feelings, which lead to actions and behaviours, some of which can be detrimental to our wellbeing and relationships.

The concept of cognitive behavioural therapy (CBT) was developed by Aaron Beck. It focuses on changing the way we think about a situation.[8] CBT is a popular form of therapy and is used by many counsellors.

A critique of this therapy is that it only addresses behaviour, not the deep pain that drives the behaviour. Nevertheless, it can be a helpful tool.

[8] "Understanding CBT," *Beck Institute*. Date of access: August 13, 2024 (https://beckinstitute.org/about/understanding-cbt).

My friend once showed me a diagram[9] that a counsellor used with her to help shift her perspective.

I used it with my child to help her work through a problem at school. The situation was so upsetting to her that she wanted to hide and never return. When we finished the process, she had come up with a solution and was prepared to go back to school in the morning.

There's no doubt that our thoughts affect our feelings and actions. Let's consider an example. My ex has a history of not paying his portion of expenses. When he was upset with me or thought I owed him money, he withheld child support. So I registered with a government program to withdraw the payments directly from his account. Currently, he owes me thousands of dollars in arrears. He refuses to pay for anything for the children, but he somehow finds the money for expensive vacations.

It came to our attention that our daughter needed braces.

As you can imagine, I dreaded asking him about this! The truth is that he doesn't want to pay for these costs and so he's always going to make the process of forcing him to pay arduous and expensive for me. I have certainly thought a lot of ugly thoughts about him, but they aren't helpful.

Here is how I filled out this diagram:

[9] Diagram is on page 34.

Describe a troubling event.

He told me he could not pay for his half of our child's braces.

Helpful		**Unhelpful**
I sent him the cost sheet & gave him the ph# to arrange payments	**THOUGHTS**	How am I going to pay for braces all by myself? Why is he so irre-sponsible?!
calm matter of fact	**FEELINGS**	worried angry
no more messages he knows theres a court order requiring him to pay half so if he doesn't pay we go through lawyers, but we'll cross that bridge when we get there	**ACTIONS**	frantic messages trying to get him to see that he needs to pay frantically trying to set up payment plans for him

ACTIVITY:

Is there a situation that is troubling you? Fill out the diagram and see if this tool helps.

SITUATION
Describe a troubling event.

_____

_____

Helpful   **Unhelpful**

_____   (**THOUGHTS**)   _____

_____   _____

_____   _____

_____   (**FEELINGS**)   _____

_____   _____

_____   _____

_____   (**ACTIONS**)   _____

_____   _____

_____   _____

God Is Trustworthy

Trust in the Lord completely,
and do not rely on your own
opinions. With all your heart
rely on him to guide you,
and he will lead you in every
decision you make.
PROVERBS 3:5 (TPT)

We can trust the Lord completely. One hundred percent! He is trustworthy because *"in him there is no darkness at all"* (1 John 1:5, NIV). It takes faith to trust in God, but it's not blind faith since we know that God is trustworthy.

We know this because Romans 8:28 tells us:

And we know that in all things God works for the good of those who love him, who have been called according to his purpose. (NIV)

In the midst of the mess, it's hard to see God's plan. We don't know all the details, and we never will, but He does. We don't know the future, but He does.

Pray for wisdom and He will give it! He is faithful.

What problems are looming over you, and what decisions do you need to make? Rely on Him because He will guide you.

My ex and I have been in and out of court for years, and we've both always been self-represented. He tried to build a parental alienation case against me. He had zero proof but plenty of allegations. I believed that God was telling me it was time to get an advocate.

I asked to consult my previous lawyer, but he was too busy. He also told me I couldn't afford him. He was right.

"Jane, you need a lawyer," a friend said to me. "How much will it cost? I'll lend you the money and it doesn't matter when you pay me back."

"Are you sure? It could be years… like, nine."

"No pressure. No strings."

Feeling grateful, I took her up on it. I called four law firms in the city, but no one was accepting new clients. Finally, I called a fifth law firm and learned that an experienced lawyer had just joined their firm the previous day. She was looking for clients.

Rest assured, beloved, that He guides me—and He guides you.

ACTIVITY:

When I was at a conference, I learned about neurographic art. According to Alexandra Vergara of the Vancouver Visual Art Foundation, the term neurographic comes from two words: neuro and graphic.[10] Neuro refers "to brain cells and connections between them and the body," and graphic refers "to the images, shapes and

---

[10] Alexandra Vergara, "The Benefits of Neurographic Art," *Vancouver Visual Art Foundation*. June 27, 2022 (https://www.vanvaf.com/post/the-benefits-of-neurographic-art).

ideas in art."[11] This type of artwork connects the unconscious to the conscious and "it is one of the most widely used psychological techniques in art therapy today."[12]

When I participated in neurographic art at the conference, we were instructed to write a problem on the back of the page, and during this process we would receive clarity.

From my perspective, I asked God a question: "Why am I getting sucked into his drama?"

Throughout the process, He gave me the answer: "You don't trust Me enough."

I was moved to tears. It hit me like a ton of bricks because I could see how this played out in my life. My ex constantly and consistently put roadblocks wherever he could. I needed to do what I could and trust God with the outcome.

Try your hand at neurographic art. For supplies, you will need plain white paper, a black marker, as well as coloured markers, crayons, or pencil crayons.

Here's what you do next:

1. Set yourself up in a quiet, comfortable spot.
2. If you desire, write your question on the back of your paper in pencil.
3. On the front, with your black marker, draw freeform lines from one edge to another, being careful not to end a line in the middle of the page. Be sure that your lines are random and unplanned. Let your marker flow!
4. Colour the resulting sections as you wish.

---

[11] Ibid.

[12] Ibid.

Wisdom Comes from God

> Don't think for a moment that
> you know it all, for wisdom
> comes when you adore him
> with undivided devotion and
> avoid everything that's wrong.
> Then you will find the healing
> refreshment your body and
> spirit long for.
> **PROVERBS 3:7-8 (TPT)**

The first ten words in today's passage pack a punch, don't they? I don't know everything, but God does. It's important to note that this verse refers to having an attitude of humility. It's not an instruction to question our reality.

There was a time when I wondered whether I knew anything at all. I wondered whether my ex and his flying monkeys were actually right. I talked to my counsellor and he said, "Jane, of course there are things you'll miss, but you're not so far off-base that you're wrong about everything."

I was baffled when I read reports from professionals who excluded evidence because they supported my ex as opposed to our daughter. I needed the confidence to believe that their conduct was unethical. I needed a measure of understanding to accept that they were people, too, and they could make mistakes. In their position of power, however, those mistakes affected our lives and could have affected the outcome of court. They needed to be held accountable.

The command to avoid everything that's wrong strikes me, too, because I've responded with snarky retorts and even hatred. I've realized that when I don't engage in the heat of the moment, or when I don't engage at all, I find healing refreshment.

I've often started a response, whether snarky or not, only to hit the delete button. I can't reason with an unreasonable person, and I can't reason with someone who's trying to be spiteful and get a rise out of me.

When I'm tempted to respond, I remind myself that I want refreshment. Actually, my body and spirit long for healing refreshment! If I live with integrity and trust God completely, relying on Him, I will find the healing refreshment I long for. Sounds good to me! I want to live with God's wisdom, trusting in Him. His refreshment sounds divine!

ACTIVITY:

My pastor held classes on conversational prayer with Jesus, and taking them was an amazing experience for me. It was a lengthy course, but the bottom line is that Jesus wants to communicate with us personally. He wants to guide and direct us. He wants us to follow Him willingly.

One day I was writing in my journal and didn't know what to ask, so I posed this question: "Lord, what do You want to tell me?"

"I have loved you with an everlasting love."

His reply brought me to tears. Even though this happened years ago, remembering it still brings tears to my eyes.

In this activity, try conversational prayer with your heavenly Father. What does He have to share with you? Often He reminds us of scripture. Other times it will be direction. Whatever He tells you, it must align with scripture, otherwise it's not Him.

For a song, I recommend "This We Know" by Elevation Worship.

He Comforts Us

He always comes alongside us
to comfort us in every suffering
so that we can come alongside
those who are in any painful
trial. We can bring them this
same comfort that God has
poured out upon us.

2 CORINTHIANS 1:4 (TPT)

In Paul's second letter to the church in Corinth, he briefly introduces himself and then jumps right in to praising God. He is the anointed One! He is worthy of our praise! He is tender-hearted. And when we go through trials, He comes alongside us to comfort us! We're not alone because God is with us.

I often find myself wondering why. Why is my ex being so difficult? Why is he watching porn? Why is he lying? Why is he so smug about hurting me and our kids? Why is he so mean, and why does he enjoy being mean? Why is this happening to me? Why did I marry him? Why didn't God stop me? This is not what I signed up for.

We don't know the answers to our questions except to say that Jesus said we will experience trouble (John 16:33). Trials are inevitable, so hopefully we use them to develop our perseverance and character (James 1:2–4). And hopefully we allow God to comfort us.

Today's passage tells us that God comforts us in our suffering so we can come alongside others in their times of need.

God is tender-hearted, compassionate, and near to the broken-hearted. The trial is here. It's not going anywhere. We can't escape it, even though, as King David wrote, he too would have loved to fly away and hide in the hills! Instead we can allow God to come beside us and comfort us. He also gives us the opportunity to come alongside others in their times of need.

Throughout this journey, I've found it hard to meet new people because I'm exhausted. My troubles are overwhelming and I'm doing all I can to pay lawyer fees, bills, and the mortgage. It's hard to be a good single parent and deal with my ex's drama. I have felt alone.

That's why I joined a support group. There are many support groups for women going through similar situations to mine—including ones hosted by Leslie Vernick, Natalie Hoffman, Patrick Doyle, and Sarah McDougal, to name a few. Often they are a safe place where we can come alongside others to offer comfort and support, and they can do the same for us.

Going through such difficult circumstances gives us empathy for others. When I was younger, I wondered why so many couples divorced. I sure didn't think it would be me one day! I thought that being a mom would be fun and easy, but I didn't think I'd have to deal with a counter-parent. I didn't think we would be going through the court system for years, that I'd be writing and reading countless affidavits and finally hiring a lawyer.

Life isn't easy for anyone. We know that life isn't without its trials, and we know God is there to comfort us so we can comfort others.

ACTIVITY:

How has God comforted you during your trials? Write a list of twenty-five ways in which God has comforted you. Thank Him.

Who around you is struggling? Write down a couple of ways in which you can help them. Is there a support group you can join? Beloved, you are not alone.

For another song, I recommend "My Prayer for You" by Alisa Turner.

Servant Leadership

But this is not your calling.
You will lead by a completely
different model. The greatest
one among you will live as
the one who is called to serve
others, because the greatest
honor and authority is reserved
for the one with the heart of
a servant. For even the Son of
Man did not come expecting to
be served but to serve and give
his life in exchange for
the salvation of many.
MATTHEW 20:26–28 (TPT)

In this passage, the mother of Zebedee's sons, James and John, wanted them to have seats of honour beside Jesus in His kingdom, but this didn't sit well with the other disciples. They all wanted a piece of the pie and they didn't want special honour given to James and John.

Jesus knew their hearts, though, and took this moment to teach them about godly leadership. In this world, kings and those in authority can be cruel, unfair, and restrict the freedoms of their subjects, but this is in opposition to how Jesus's followers lead. Even Jesus didn't assume such power!

I will preface this by noting that I don't believe the Bible teaches that a husband has power over his wife. Matthew 20 speaks to how Christians embody leadership. Jesus used the example of the relationship between a king and his subject. In such a relationship, there is little mutuality; the onus is on the king to guard himself against the desire for oppressive power.

This passage doesn't talk about a husband-wife relationship. We know this because the Bible elsewhere speaks of mutuality in marriage (1 Corinthians 7:3–4, Ephesians 5:21). But that is another devotional.

In Matthew 20, Jesus teaches about servant leadership. Many husbands who teach headship and submission in the home function as the kings and rulers of this world; they are cruel and unfair, restricting freedoms and treating their wives as subjects.

Beloved, this should not be. God's style of leadership is servant leadership, not tyranny or dictatorship. Some men claim they have a God-given right to be leaders of the home, but they resemble the kings and rulers of this world. If headship and submission is their doctrine, if they believe the husband is head of the home, then at the very least they should adopt a godly style of leadership. But many don't. Tragically, they do exactly what Jesus told the disciples not to do!

In Jesus's teaching, we see that leadership has never been an excuse for the abuse of power. A servant leader doesn't demand submission or require the final say in all decisions. A godly leader has a servant's heart, meaning that they genuinely care. A husband's desire to rule over his wife comes from pride, selfishness, and a desire to control; it doesn't come from scripture.

ACTIVITY:

Spend some time journaling about godly leadership. In your circles, how do Christian leaders lead? How do you lead? How does Jesus describe a leader? Does your husband claim to be your leader? How does this play out in your relationship? What happens when you offer an opinion? Have you been too passive? Have you been assertive? Do you pay a price when you're assertive? Has your husband been aggressive?

Lots of questions, I know. Spend some time exploring servant leadership. It's not an oxymoron!

Selfishness Makes a Counter-Parent

> Do nothing from selfish
> ambition or conceit, but in
> humility count others more
> significant than yourselves. Let
> each of you look not only to his
> own interests, but also to the
> interests of others.
> **PHILIPPIANS 2:3–4 (ESV)**

This passage makes me think about co-parenting versus counter-parenting. Co-parenting is about having a partnership focused on the well-being of the children. A counter-parent is a selfish parent who makes decisions to spite the other parent.

One summer I planned to take the children to a week-long summer camp. I asked my ex whether I could have them a few hours earlier on the day we were scheduled to leave. He agreed.

But a few hours before I was supposed to pick them up, he changed his mind. As it turned out, he had changed his mind for no other reason than that he could. He had no plans; they just watched TV all afternoon.

This meant I later had to drive for hours with my exhausted children through the pitch-black countryside. Thankfully it wasn't raining and we didn't have car trouble!

It also meant that someone at the camp needed to meet us at midnight to show us to our rooms. While exhausted, we had to find our beds in the dark and set them up without disturbing the sleeping campers in our cabin.

Examples like this one are commonplace with a counter-parent. Perhaps you're dealing with a counter-parent, too. It is impossible to co-parent with a person who's unwilling to consider another person's needs.

Today's passage is also an admonishment, warning me not to become a counter-parent myself. When my ex asks for a favour, I could let spite kick in and refuse to budge just because I can. But that's not helpful.

The children wanted to go to a birthday party on my time for a friend who attends their father's church. I hated the idea of giving up a Saturday afternoon with my children because my ex could have easily shown up at the party. But I called a friend, and she gave me a perspective shift. This was about the children.

In the privacy of my bedroom, I screamed into my pillow and flailed my arms and legs. It was so unfair! In the end, the children had a great time at the birthday party and I had some time alone.

A counter-parent won't consider the needs of another person, even their own children. I have come to terms with the fact that my ex will not negotiate. When I find myself feeling hopeful that he's finally negotiating, I realize that it's a pretence; he will renege after he gets what he wants. It has happened time and time again.

I have certainly been too accommodating. At times I bend over backwards to accommodate everyone, but my back is getting sore! I need to strengthen my backbone. It's my job to consider what's in the best interests of the children and me, and to say no when I need to. This is hard because there's always a price for saying no. I need to hold firmly to my no, even when my ex badgers me and tries to manipulate me.

I'm learning that considering my needs isn't wrong. In fact, I must acknowledge that I have needs. I matter, too.

ACTIVITY:

Does your abusive man's selfishness drive you bananas? Have you ever tried screaming into a pillow? Try it! We need a physical release of the tension. Screaming into a pillow is quick and easy. Maybe you want to head outside and run some stairs, take a kick-boxing class, invest in a punching bag, beat your chest, or dance in your living room. Whatever it is, do something that requires you to physically release that tension. You'll feel better.

What About Anger?

A soft answer turns away wrath,
but a harsh word stirs up anger.
PROVERBS 15:1 (ESV)

Be angry, and yet do not sin; do
not let the sun go down
on your anger...
EPHESIANS 4:26 (NASB)

I've filed complaints about police officers. When an officer I spoke to was understanding and calm, it helped me remain calm. If an officer was harsh and unreasonable, I got angrier unless I purposefully decided to listen and remain calm. If I was accusatory, the officer got defensive. When we both listened and remained calm, the matter got addressed through discussion.

I thought the same principle would apply to my ex. I thought that if I spoke calmly to him, he'd calm down, but this isn't true of him. He is always in control of his emotions! If he wants to be loud and intimidating, he is. If he wants to be quiet and intimidating, he can do that, too. It amazes me how cool as a cucumber he can remain while taunting me. This is still anger, but it puts him in the position to point the finger at me.

I thought that if I matched or reacted to his anger, he would escalate. But when I matched him, I saw that gleam in his eye betraying his glee.

I've run the gamut in terms of how I broach topics with him. I could spend hours praying about my words and tone or I could just let the words flow. Unfortunately, I played into his games when I let them flow. I feel way better about myself when I respond calmly, or when I don't respond at all.

You may not have heard this, but you have permission to be angry. Your destructive man's manipulative words and actions naturally stir up anger in you. Likely, he has committed many injustices against you and your children, and of course this infuriates you as a wife and mother! Anger can spur us on to take corrective action, even legal action.

My ex shamed me for being angry even when I wasn't angry. I was shamed when I spoke with passion, when I had an opinion, and when I had an idea for how we could do something better. I wasn't allowed to complain. If I showed any emotion other than happiness and support, he'd let me know how ungodly I was behaving.

But here's the thing: sin makes God angry, too.

While anger is appropriate at times, we don't have permission to sin when we're angry, and we don't have permission to get stuck there. It takes time and effort to work through anger.

I have certainly felt angry. And with the help of my Square Squad, I've taken legal steps to correct injustices. I've also let anger fester. Injustice upon injustice for years can be infuriating!

To be clear, my angry responses to his provocations are merely fuel for his smear campaigns. Truth be told, he doesn't need anything from me to create a smear campaign, because he has no qualms about lying. But I make his task easier when I react poorly.

It's also easier in court when I can show that I've followed the rules and have been respectful.

I try to resolve my anger with him before a day is done, but that can be impossible. It can be impossible to obtain resolution with a destructive person because they're not interested in solving problems. Circular conversations that make you feel unhinged are fun for them.

I saw this firsthand one day when he was badgering me. He had that disgusting smug smile plastered on his face.

"Why is this fun for you?" I asked.

No answer. He just shot that smug smile in my direction.

It was awful to live with someone who took pleasure in provoking me and then pointing the finger.

Does that kind of behaviour fire you up? Of course it does, because it's wicked. I had to learn how to deal with the anger that was stuck in my chest.

ACTIVITY:

Anger is described as a secondary emotion because it is generally a result of other emotions. Anger may be expressed as aggression, annoyance, criticism, frustration, hatred, hostility, irritation, and rage.

Following is a list to help you identify some of the feelings lingering beneath the surface.

Anxiety	Fear	Hurt	Pain	Stress
Betrayal	Foolish	Injustice	Regret	Threatened
Contempt	Grief	Jealous	Rejected	Unloved
Disappointment	Guilt	Lonely	Sadness	Weak
Embarrassment	Helpless	Overwhelmed	Shame	Worry

Circle some of your underlying feelings. Is this list missing anything? Write down your feelings along with the events that have triggered them.

Make no mistake: the things your husband has done are wicked, and you have reason to feel angry. His actions make God angry, too!

You are God's precious child and He loves you. Imagine that you're resting in His arms, or imagine that the hosts of heaven are ready to be unleashed! God absolutely hates injustice. Vengeance is His. He will repay.

God Will Repay

> Dear friends, never take
> revenge. Leave that to the
> righteous anger of God. For
> the Scriptures say, "I will take
> revenge; I will pay them back,"
> says the Lord.
> **ROMANS 12:19 (NLT)**

I was curious how many times in the Bible God says that vengeance is His and He will repay. After researching the question, I found the answer: one hundred times. That is quite a promise!

Vengeance is the act of responding to an injury with injury.[13] Some people say that revenge feels good, but planning and taking revenge is shortsighted. Even though it may feel exciting in the moment, we will suffer the consequences.[14]

God takes the infractions committed by these destructive men seriously. We know the list of seven things that are an abomination to God (Proverbs 6:16–19). We also know that no sacrifice remains for those who deliberately continue to sin even after knowing the truth (Hebrews 10:26–27). We know that a husband

---

[13] "Vengeance," *Merriam-Webster*. Date of access: September 10, 2024 (https://www.merriam-webster.com/dictionary/vengeance).

[14] Geoff Beattie, "Revenge: The Neuroscience of Why It Feels Good in the Moment, but May Be a Bad Idea in the Long Run," *The Conversation*. January 26, 2022 (https://theconversation.com/revenge-the-neuroscience-of-why-it-feels-good-in-the-moment-but-may-be-a-bad-idea-in-the-long-run-175747).

who refuses to care for his family is worse than an unbeliever (1 Timothy 5:8). These sins make God burn with righteous anger.

We don't need to seek revenge, because it's the Lord's job and eventually they will expose themselves. The Lord states in Deuteronomy 32:35, *"It is mine to avenge; I will repay. In due time their foot will slip"* (NIV). Eventually their masks will crack and fall. They cannot masquerade forever.

It sure is tempting to plan revenge, but Romans 12:21 tells us:

Do not be overcome by evil, but overcome evil with good. (NIV)

Just as my ex's actions are his responsibility, my actions are mine. I want to hold my head high, knowing that I haven't stepped out of line. I want to live a life above reproach. I want to be a good example to my children.

Let God unleash His righteous anger on the wrongdoer. He's got your back.

ACTIVITY:
So what do we do with these feelings we're left with? Remember King David's imprecatory prayers? He prayed that God would hold wrongdoers accountable and they would be severely punished. David never shied away from his strong emotions, and God didn't ask him to.

While we may feel strong emotions, we don't have to act on them.

We do need to live differently than the world. Though we feel our anger, we do not sin. Godly love and godly anger can exist in the same person. It's not loving to let repeated offences slide; it's enabling.

God hates sin and promises to repay it.

The bottom line is that King David said his piece and left the results in God's capable hands.

While we don't act on these emotions, we do acknowledge them. When a friend was in group therapy, they wrote rage letters. A letter can be a safe way to express everything you've been holding in.

If you're comfortable, write a rage letter. Who do you have anger in your heart towards? If I'm honest, I have anger towards a therapist, police officers, social workers, family members, and former friends. Maybe you had a terrible lawyer or an unfair judge. Take a moment to reflect on who wronged you, their actions that need to be punished, and how you think they should be punished. What consequences have you or your children suffered as a result of their actions? There is no need to censor yourself. Let it all out!

When you're finished, destroy the paper and leave it in God's capable hands. He is with you.

For a song, I suggest listening to "He Is with Us" by Love & the Outcome.

Don't Worry

Therefore I tell you, do not
worry about your life, what you
will eat or drink; or about your
body, what you will wear. Is not
life more than food, and the
body more than clothes? Look
at the birds of the air; they do
not sow or reap or store away
in barns, and yet your heavenly
Father feeds them. Are you not
much more valuable than they?
Can any one of you by worrying
add a single hour to your life?
…Therefore do not worry
about tomorrow, for tomorrow
will worry about itself. Each day
has enough trouble of its own.

MATTHEW 6:25-27, 34 (NIV)

I have so many things to worry about. Will my kids be safe with
my ex today? What will the judge say? How will I pay for a lawyer? Will I get the house? How will I buy groceries this month?
Should I go back to school to get a better job—and if I do, will I
be able to find a job in that field? If I say such-and-such to him,
how will he react? Why doesn't that person like me anymore?

What did he say to her? How will he disparage me to my children today? The hot water tank needs to be replaced, but how will I pay for it? Will the repair man overcharge me?

These are some of the worries on my list. What are some of the worries on your list?

Even when the Lord has given me answers to bring me peace, I still worry! Can you believe it?

I wish that I had the faith to just believe and rest knowing that God will provide. He knows exactly what my kids and I need at exactly the right time. He provides everything I need, and oftentimes even things that I merely want!

Towards the end of my marriage, I was hired for a contract position at a local company. I enjoyed the work and it went well.

After the separation, I felt like I should be working even though God told me I needed to rest. I felt guilty and lazy, so I applied for positions I was qualified for but didn't get a single interview.

After a couple of months, a friend offered me a position at their business. This was a healing time for me. After a few months, a colleague who knew me from the contract position a year earlier told me that a new position was being created and encouraged me to apply. I did, and I was hired. This job paid almost double the wage I made currently.

This spring, I'm receiving my five-year award.

Undoubtedly, every job is a gift from God, and my current job is no exception. I have an understanding supervisor. I have benefits. I was able to take a personal leave with full pay when dealing with court and my ex was overwhelming. God knew exactly what

I needed years before I knew I needed it, and He created a solution at just the right time.

We can worry, but it's crippling. It destroys us. Worry and stress negatively affect our body, mood, and behaviour. When it affects our bodies, we can suffer from headaches, lack of sleep, and a weakened immune system. When it affects our mood, we can suffer from anxiety, feelings of overwhelm, and a lack of motivation. When it affects our behaviours, we can turn to substances, isolation, and angry outbursts.[15]

These lists certainly aren't exhaustive. Jesus was right! Worrying does not add to my life; it robs me!

I've lost so much by worrying, and I can't get that time back. I want to rest knowing that I am valuable to Him. If He provides for the birds of the air, He will surely provide for me and my children. He will provide for you, too!

I sure don't want to spend another minute worrying. I'll walk into the next court appearance prepared and with my confidence placed securely in Him because, come what may, I am safe in His arms, and so are my children. And so are you.

ACTIVITY:
How has God provided for you? Take the time to write down at least thirty ways in which God has provided for you. Let this list build your faith. And when you begin to doubt, reread it. God wants to give you good gifts! He wants to provide exactly the

---

[15] "Stress Symptoms: Effects on Your Body and Behaviour," The Mayo Clinic, August 10, 2023, https://www.mayoclinic.org/healthy-lifestyle/stress-management/in-depth/stress-symptoms/art-20050987

right gift at exactly the right time. You are so valuable! You are His prized creation!

Do you need a song to remind you? I recommend "Treasure of You" by Steven Curtis Chapman.

Live at Peace

If possible, so far as it depends
on you, live peaceably with all.
ROMANS 12:18 (ESV)

What does it look like to live peaceably with men like my ex? I've learned that the normal rules don't apply. I used to JADE—justify, argue, defend, and explain—hoping that we would be able to have reasonable conversations. It never happened. He's never said, "Oh, that's a great point, Jane. I didn't think about that!" He's never appreciated feedback from anyone, and he never will.

I realized that if I asked him for what I wanted—for example, for him to watch less porn—he'd watch just as much as ever, or more. When I asked him to put safeguards on the computer, he refused. I finally realized that if I asked him not to do something, he would do it more. If I asked him to do something, he would refuse.

I realized that I needed to stop wasting my precious time and energy. Living peaceably with him means no contact—as little as possible and through my lawyer if possible. It means offering no explanations and making no attempts at negotiation. It's hard, I know, but he's not an average sinner.

What about living peacefully with his flying monkeys? This is also impossible. They have believed his lies and there's no going back. I want them to hear my side of the story, but they won't. I know because I've tried. When I've tried to have conversations with these people, many of whom are family members, they would just repeat back his narrative. The only way they'll change their minds is if they become direct recipients of his maltreatment. Even then, there's no guarantee.

In an attempt to live at peace and to settle outside of court, some people suggested mediation with a third party. Judges and lawyers often recommend professional mediators. Mediation requires willing participants, though. If the other party isn't willing to see your perspective, the process won't work. When my ex agreed to a solution in mediation, he never followed through with that agreement. It was much better for him to appear cooperative at first and then ignore it. Mediated agreements aren't legally binding, so he would have required a court order to follow through.

I refused mediation because it had been futile. He turned this around on me by saying that I was creating high conflict and wasting money and resources that should have gone to the children.

Peace is impossible with a person like my ex.

The same is true of counselling sessions. I would arrange these sessions and drag him there kicking and screaming, only for him to appear peaceable and reasonable with the counsellor. But as soon as we'd step out the door, he would be back to his normal self.

My ex's image was everything to him. He wrote very selfish emails to my lawyer, to the children's lawyer, and affidavits and applications to the court. After just a few months, my lawyer realized that he was only concerned for himself.

I had to pay for every email he sent my lawyer and every reply she sent back, and eventually I got tired of it. Finally, I sent him a message: "Do you realize how selfish you look in your correspondence?" Apparently he didn't realize it, but he didn't want to look selfish, so the next emails he sent were one-sentence long and straight to the point. This gave me peace, at least for a time, but his good behaviour was short-lived!

It's impossible to have a peaceful relationship with someone who's only interested in control and manipulation to get their way. So what can we do to have peace?

ACTIVITY:

Here are some questions to answer in your journal. How much energy have you dedicated to trying to reason or negotiate with the destructive man in your life? What has he taught you about reasoning with him? Do your interactions give you resolution and peace or more frustration? How can you live at peace with him and his flying monkeys? Sometimes superficial contact with flying monkeys is possible; other times it's not.

I've encountered helpful acronyms online to help navigate these high conflict relationships and live in peace. It's so hard not to get sucked in, but we can do it. It's worth it. I always regret when I don't follow these acronyms.

- KISS: Keep It Simple, Sister!
- BIFF: Brief, Informative, Friendly, Firm
- and don't JADE: Justify, Argue, Defend, Engage

I sometimes feel rude when I get straight to the point, especially if my ex is trying to engage with me. He makes his responses seem friendly on the surface. He calls me Sweetheart in messages.

He sends early morning messages praying that I'll have a blessed day. He messages me to tell me that God loves me and he's praying for me.

God understands people like my ex. Psalm 55:21 says, *"His words are as smooth as butter, but in his heart is war. His words are as soothing as lotion, but underneath are daggers!"* (NLT) I need to be okay with being the one who appears cold in messages. If he uses them to show people how kind he was to me and prove how resistant I am to his affections, so be it.

Today's activity is to decide to maintain your peace by following these tips: KISS, BIFF, and don't JADE.

God Guides Us

I hear the Lord saying, "I will
stay close to you, instructing
and guiding you along the
pathway for your life. I will
advise you along the way and
lead you forth with my eyes
as your guide. So don't make
it difficult; don't be stubborn
when I take you where you've
not been before. Don't make
me tug you and pull you along.
Just come with me!"

PSALM 32:8–9 (TPT)

This passage encourages me. I love the promise that God will stay close to me and guide me along the best pathway for my life.

I've thought of this in terms of my life after divorce, but now I see that it also includes my life before divorce. He has stayed close to me throughout my entire life. This life isn't free of trouble, but when I encounter trouble He guides and leads me. Was my marriage a big mistake? I made the best decision with the information I had at the time, being the person I was. Through it all, God has been my guide.

I also want to be an easy student—you know, an excellent student, a pleasure to have in class! I don't want to be stubborn and sit in self-pity or regret. I want to be willing and teachable.

When I come upon choppy waters in uncharted seas with no idea of what's coming next, I can assign the nervousness I feel in the pit of my stomach to fear and trepidation, or I can assign it to excitement and anticipation to see where God is leading me!

If I capsize, He's there to save me. I won't drown. If I manage to stay in the boat, He's there with me, too. Either way, He's with me through the storm and will bring me to the other side.

The same is true for you, beloved. Trust that He will guide you.

ACTIVITY:

God promises to stay close, leading and guiding you. Follow Him down the best pathway for your life! Do the next right thing. If you don't feel Him leading you, maybe the best thing to do is wait. Rest assured that even though the future is uncertain, He illuminates your next steps.

It can be hard not to freeze in indecision at important points in our lives, because the decisions we make can have a lasting impact on us and our loved ones. But don't let fear hold you captive. If you make a poor decision, you made the best decision you could at the time. Now you have the information you need to adjust.

In this journalling activity, consider these questions. How has God guided you? How is He guiding you now?

Here are a couple of songs that encouraged me: "God Is in Control" by Twila Paris and "Everything Is in Your Hands" by Vineyard Music. Feel free to listen, stretch, dance, or doodle in your journal.

Don't Get Weary of Taking the High Road

> Those who live only to satisfy
> their own sinful nature will
> harvest decay and death from
> that sinful nature. But those
> who live to please the Spirit will
> harvest everlasting life from the
> Spirit. So let's not get tired of
> doing what is good. At just the
> right time we will reap a harvest
> of blessing if we don't give up.
>
> **GALATIANS 6:8–9 (NLT)**

One of the biggest lies I've heard in Christian teaching is that I'm responsible for my ex's sin: his porn, his laziness, his lies, his cheating, his manipulations, and his cruel treatment of me and the children. For someone who holds this opinion, if I'm not solely responsible then I definitely contributed to his sin. They ask, why would he cheat or look at porn if he was satisfied at home?

These are lies from the pit of hell. If my ex chooses to live in sin, it's on him. If I choose to live in sin, it's on me. If he chooses to sin, he suffers the painful consequences. And let's face it: the kids and I do, too.

In fact, I believe that my failed marriage is the natural consequence of my ex living out of his sinful nature. Bold words, I know! I've heard the objection: "You're not perfect, Jane!" It's true. I'm not perfect. No one is. But neither is an abuser, and an abuser typically isn't an ordinary sinner who accepts feedback, self-reflects, and changes their behaviour.

On the other hand, if he chooses to live in the Spirit, there will be a harvest of everlasting life from the Spirit! If I choose to live in the Spirit, that will be my reward as well!

So, dear ones, let's persevere in doing what is right. If we do, there will be a reward. I know that it's not always easy to do the right thing, though. I haven't always taken the high road.

On a Sunday after my ex was being particularly impossible, I called his mother and told her that she had raised a monster. What did I think that would accomplish? Did I think she was actually going to say, "Yes, you're right. I'm sorry, Jane. I enabled him to be an entitled jerk"? No. I merely supported her existing position, that I was completely unreasonable and in need of much prayer.

At my friend's prompting, I called her back to apologize. She didn't answer, so I left a message. Friends, it was like drinking vinegar!

Reaping a harvest takes time. When I plant corn in our garden, I have to wait three months to harvest it. When I plant basil, I can harvest it much sooner. The point is that I have to be patient. I have to keep doing the right thing over and over. The harvest will come at just the right time.

Maybe my relationships will be restored. I would love that! Maybe I won't give my ex inspiration for another attack on my character. Maybe I'll reduce my interactions with him. Maybe I won't embarrass myself. Who knows what the rewards will be?

Don't give up! Press on! Do the right thing and apologize when you don't.

ACTIVITY:

Having to deal with a destructive ex, hurtful family members, and crazy flying monkeys causes significant amounts of stress to build up. What do I do with it?

I've always been averse to cold water, so I've never been tempted to participate in a polar bear plunge. I've thought that people who take the plunge must be a bit crazy!

As it turns out, exposure to cold stimulates our vagus nerve and helps us calm down. In fact, a study has shown that while there are significant safety considerations, immersing oneself in cold water can significantly improve your mood.[16]

Come to think of it, of all the pictures I've seen of participants emerging from frigid waters, there is not a frown in sight!

I started out with baby steps. While at the beach, my friend told me about the benefits of submerging in cold water. She encouraged me to give it a try, but I'm such a chicken that I only submerged my toes—and that was into little puddles that had been warmed by the sun! It clearly wasn't enough to reap any benefits.

I can, however, bear splashing cold water on my face, although from what I've read that isn't enough either. You have to actually submerge your face in cold water.

---

[16] "Can Cold Water Really Help Alleviate Anxiety?" *Wellin5*. Date of access: August 14, 2024 (https://wellin5.ca/how-cold-water-immersion-can-improve-mental-health).

Today, consider stimulating your vagus nerve with cold water: dip your body, submerge your face, apply a cold compress to the back of your neck, or hold an ice cube to your skin. Maybe you'll be braver, and more relaxed, than I am!

You Matter, Too!

> Husbands have the obligation
> of loving and caring for their
> wives the same way they love
> and care for their own bodies,
> for to love your wife is to love
> your own self. No one abuses
> his own body, but pampers it—
> serving and satisfying its needs.
> That's exactly what Christ does
> for his church!
>
> **EPHESIANS 5:28-29 (TPT)**

I've heard a lot about how wives should submit to their husbands. In fact, when I was a teen my dad told my mom during an argument that she was supposed to submit to him.

I interjected, "Actually, Ephesians 5:21 says to submit one to another."

He turned to me. "Jane, if you ever get married, you won't be married for more than a year!"

Well, my marriage lasted nearly twelve years! Dare I say it: my dad's command for my mom to submit to him came from a place of selfishness and pride, not love.

I heard my dad proclaim the doctrine of headship and submission, but I never heard him quote today's verse. My ex never quoted it either. The New American Standard Version uses the words *nourish* and *cherish,* saying that a husband is supposed to nourish and cherish his wife. My ex didn't nourish or cherish me. But make no mistake: I was unquestionably expected to nourish and cherish him and be at his beck and call. My needs didn't matter to him.

When the kids were young and I was up with them at all hours of the night and cleaning until 1:00 a.m., I felt exhausted. If I napped, he would wake me up since I had work to do and supper to make! However, he phrased it as concern for me; if I napped, I wouldn't be able to sleep at night.

Truth be told, I couldn't sleep at night either! Many times he kept me up into the wee hours of the morning complaining about something I had or hadn't done. He would watch porn in the middle of the night and then wake me up to finish off because I was his wife and that was my obligation.

He deprived me of a basic need—sleep—for so many years. After our separation, I was so thankful to have the bed to myself so I could sleep!

Even though I've heard people teach that this passage of scripture supports the notion that a husband rules over his wife just as Christ rules over the church, it does not teach that. The comparison to Christ doesn't give a husband the role of unquestionable ruler over his wife. The comparison is meant to show us that we love one another because He first loved us (1 John 4:19). Husbands love because Christ loves. The passage doesn't teach that a husband is superior to his wife. Rather, it teaches that a husband should love his wife, care for her, and lay his life down for her.

Beloved, you are not second rate. You matter, too! A marriage in which you are required to serve and satisfy the needs and desires of your husband, with no thought to your own needs, let alone desires, is built on false doctrine. It's a self-serving doctrine that has no place in a Christian marriage.

Paul speaks of mutuality in marriage (1 Corinthians 7:1–3). He also speaks of unity in the body of Christ. All parts of the body of Christ are important. An eye, for example, cannot say to the hand, *"I don't need you!"* (1 Corinthians 12:21) The body of Christ works together and knows that each part has value.

This biblical teaching isn't suddenly void in marriage. God is painting a beautiful picture of a partnership in which both parties are concerned about the needs of the other—a partnership where love reigns.

ACTIVITY:

I learned about the following scale from Leslie Vernick, and it has been invaluable to me. In fact, I highly recommend taking any class with her!

Here's the scale:

-3   -2   -1   0   +1   +2   +3

On this scale, the numbers range from -3 on the low end to +3 on the high end. A person who doesn't think about their own needs and desires is at -3. That was me. I actually prided myself on not having any needs. I didn't want to be a bother, so

I accommodated others at every opportunity. I was also overly concerned about appearing selfish.

On the opposite end of the scale is a person who only thinks of their own needs and desires. This represents my ex.

A healthy place for both parties to be is in the middle, from -1 to +1. As Philippians 2:4 says, *"Do not merely look out for your own personal interests, but also for the interests of others"* (NASB).

Where do you see yourself on this scale? If you're at -3, as I was, what are some ways in which you can become more assertive? The first step is recognizing that you do have needs, and they're just as important as your husband's. Write down some of your needs and wants. Remember, you matter, too!

The Lord Hears Your Prayers

The Lord is far from the wicked,
but he hears the prayer
of the righteous.
PROVERBS 15:29 (NIV)

Last night I had coffee with a dear friend. As we shared our stories, she told me that she often stays awake at night praying that God would give me the strength and courage to press on. I told her that I know He answers her prayers.

Here's one example. I knew my ex was trying to build a case of child alienation against me, but I didn't know how to combat it. I woke up one morning with a start, believing that God had told me to book an appointment with a particular lawyer.

I was disappointed that the only time this lawyer had available was three weeks away, but I waited.

Then, four days before my appointment, I received my ex's court application and affidavit. He wanted sole parenting time for our youngest child; according to him, I was turning her against him.

When the lawyer saw these dates, he asked, "But didn't you book this appointment weeks ago?"

"Yes, I did," I acknowledged.

The lawyer then gave me advice on how to write my response affidavit.

Rest assured, dear one, that God knows the future. I was disappointed about having to wait so long for the meeting with this lawyer, but God knew what was coming. He prompted me to call right when I needed to. In fact, the lawyer told me in the meeting that I had called just in time, since his caseload was almost at capacity. When I called, they had been on the verge of starting to turn clients away.

Beloved, He will give you wisdom every step of the way. He hears you when you pray, and He hears your friends when they pray.

ACTIVITY:

How has God answered your prayers or your friends' prayers for you? How has He given you the desires of your heart? Write your answers in your journal.

Restoration Is Impossible without Repentance

The Lord is close to all whose
hearts are crushed by pain, and
he is always ready to restore
the repentant one.
PSALM 34:18 (TPT)

This verse reminds me of the occasion when the prophet Nathan confronted King David about the sin he had committed against Bathsheba and her husband. David didn't deny, deflect, or minimize his actions, nor did he shift the blame onto Bathsheba. Nope. He acknowledged what he had done and was broken over it.

To be honest, David isn't my favourite guy in the Bible. In my opinion, he was a terrible husband and father, but he was a man after God's own heart because he admitted when he messed up. Feeling crushed, he repented and turned his life around, accepting the consequences.

Even though he caused his own pain by choosing to sin and then sinning again by covering it up, the Lord was near to him and restored him. Why? Because David was repentant.

We serve a compassionate God! He knows that we sin and will always restore us when we come to Him, broken and contrite. Ladies, let this be us!

It's clear that restoration is impossible without repentance. If David had been dishonest, unwilling to accept feedback, and unrepentant, he wouldn't have been restored. Simple as that. He would have carried on in his muck, but that wasn't his heart. He didn't want to stay stuck in his muck. He wasn't perfect, but he was repentant.

When I got married, I thought my husband and I were going to be a powerhouse ministry couple. It didn't happen. I often prayed that God would soften his heart, and I was confused when he didn't change even though I believed that God could change anyone and no one was beyond His reach.

This verse explains why my ex never changed: he wasn't repentant. Even when the evidence was staring him right in the face, he was defensive, dishonest, unwilling to accept feedback, and unrepentant. He claimed to be a Christian and gave that outward appearance, but sadly his heart was, and is, far from the Lord. It was such a hard reality to accept.

God is always ready to restore the repentant one, but my ex was and is content in his muck. We, beloved, are not. May our prayer always be: *"Cleanse me with hyssop, and I will be clean; wash me, and I will be whiter than snow"* (Psalm 51:7, NIV).

ACTIVITY:

Does the destructive man in your life confess his sins of his own volition or do you uncover it? If you uncover it and confront him, what is his response? Does he care that his behaviour hurts you? Does he act with supposed godliness in public and bare his teeth at home? Does he seek accountability for himself? The answers to these questions will demonstrate whether he is repentant.

These destructive relationships are stressful, to say the least. Oftentimes I feel tension and stress stuck in my body. Do you feel it in your body?

There is a lot of information online about the vagus nerve. Kati Morton explains that it's part of the parasympathetic nervous system and, when stimulated, helps us relax. She teaches five easy ways to stimulate the vagus nerve. Feel free to watch her video and choose one of the methods to stimulate your vagus nerve and help your body relax.[17]

---

[17] Kati Morton, "5 Easy Ways to Stimulate the Vagus Nerve," YouTube. May 17, 2021 (https://www.youtube.com/watch?v=fSN2CeDkslg).

Perspective Shift

My fellow believers, when it
seems as though you are facing
nothing but difficulties, see it
as an invaluable opportunity
to experience the greatest joy
that you can! For you know
that when your faith is tested
it stirs up in you the power of
endurance. And then as your
endurance grows even stronger,
it will release perfection into
every part of your being until
there is nothing missing and
nothing lacking.

JAMES 1:2–4 (TPT)

When I was being bombarded with struggle after struggle, I wanted to make it stop. I wanted God to stop it. I wanted my ex to stop it. But it didn't stop. Even after a tumultuous marriage, ugly separation, and high-conflict divorce, it still hasn't stopped. It has changed, but it hasn't stopped.

I certainly didn't see my difficulties as invaluable opportunities to experience the greatest joy! I saw my difficulties as the death of my dreams.

I've often heard that joy isn't a synonym for happiness. The Bible Project has a definition that captures what I've been taught: "Biblical joy is more than a happy feeling. It's a lasting emotion that comes from the choice to trust that God will fulfill his promises."[18]

I have a choice to make. I can choose to believe that God will fulfill His promises, or I can choose to stay stuck in my circumstances. The promise in this passage is that my trials will produce powerful endurance and that powerful endurance will make me mature and complete. I like the sound of this!

Another thing that strikes me about this verse is that it doesn't dismiss our trials. Our trials are real, dear one. God never shies away from acknowledging that there are hard times in life. Minimizing the severity of our trials minimizes God's redemptive work in our lives.

In this passage, James says that we need a perspective shift. Joy isn't a direct result of our struggles. Our joy rests in knowing that when our faith is tested and perseverance developed, we can keep going and become mature. Don't waste these trials. Press on!

ACTIVITY:

What is your perspective? Are you weighed down by circumstances? It is understandable. James admonishes us to use these challenges to develop perseverance and maturity, and that, beloved, is exciting!

Today's challenge is to be active. Not only is it good for your body, it's also good for your brain!

[18] "Chara/Joy," *Bible Project*. December 14, 2017 (https://bibleproject.com/explore/video/chara-joy).

What's your favourite kind of exercise? You can head outside for a walk or run, go to the park with your kids, or visit the gym. I have a simple home gym in my basement and I love my workouts there. I can feel ready to take on the world in as little as four minutes! Get that heartrate up![19]

---

[19] If you're physically able and have your doctor's permission.

Ask God for Wisdom

And if anyone longs to be wise,
ask God for wisdom and he will
give it! He won't see your lack
of wisdom as an opportunity to
scold you over your failures but
he will overwhelm your failures
with his generous grace. Just
make sure you ask empowered
by confident faith without
doubting that you will receive.
JAMES 1:5–6 (TPT)

While I was considering leaving, my ex took a chunk of money out of our account. As a stay-at-home mom, I was scared. I had no income and I didn't know what he was planning.

I called a couple of friends who were also afraid for me. Together we talked about withdrawing some money for myself, but I didn't have peace about it.

Later I headed out to visit my mom. Along the way, I drove past the bank. Again, I didn't have peace about stopping there to withdraw cash.

On my way home, I took the exit for the bank, but I felt uneasy. Soon I came to the intersection where I had to make a decision: I could go straight to the bank or turn right to return home.

"Okay, Lord, this is it," I prayed. "What should I do?"

"Turn."

So I turned.

When I called my friend and told her the story, she said, "Shut up! No way! This is the scripture passage I'm reading right now."

It came from John 10:27–28: *"My sheep listen to My voice, and I know them, and they follow Me; and I give them eternal life, and they will never perish; and no one will snatch them out of My hand"* (NASB).

The Lord had given me wisdom to turn right. He also gave me assurance that I was His child.

This happened at the beginning of the end of my marriage.

After the police eventually served him the emergency protection order (EPO) and escorted him to our home to get his belongings, we were officially headed down the road of divorce.

"Why are you doing this?" his sister asked. "I want to see you in heaven one day."

Her implication was clear: if I got divorced, I wouldn't go to heaven. But God had already given me the assurance that I belong to Him.

Sadly, she wasn't the only family member to make such comments, but the wisdom God gave me has been my anchor.

ACTIVITY:

God gives us wisdom when we ask. How has God given you wisdom? What are you curious about? Ask Him and see what He says. Write your thoughts and answers in your journal.

God Gives Good Gifts

Which of you, if your son
asks for bread, will give him a
stone? Or if he asks for a fish,
will give him a snake? If you,
then, though you are evil, know
how to give good gifts to your
children, how much more will
your Father in heaven give good
gifts to those who ask him!

MATTHEW 7:9–11 (NIV)

God gives good gifts. He's our Father and He wants the best for us.

My ex and I purchased our first house about a year before we separated. After my children and I went to stay at a women's shelter and I applied for an EPO, my ex was no longer allowed to live in that home. I wanted the children and I to remain there to give them consistency.

While I was praying about the house, God told me that He was going to give it to me. I didn't know if He meant long-term or just during the EPO hearings.

We went to court several times, and I felt nervous each time. In the end, the judge granted me exclusive possession of the home for a year.

When I let my lawyer know that I wanted to purchase the house, he told me that it would be impossible. But he handed me a business card anyway.

"Call this broker," the lawyer said. "Then you'll know for sure that it's impossible."

So I called the broker and she told me that she *could* make the numbers work.

Later, as I was signing the papers for my very first mortgage, my lawyer said, "This is only by the grace of God."

It certainly was.

I'm sure my emotional rollercoaster ride could have been less terrifying if I had rested in God's promise to me from the beginning. In the end, He gave me possession of my first home on February 14, 2020. It was God's Valentine's Day gift to me. The year is special to me, too. 2020: perfect vision. I'm forever grateful.

ACTIVITY:

What has God given you? Write it down. What do you want? Is it wild and crazy? Is it impossible? Ask Him.

You know that look on your child's face when you've given them a special gift that touches their heart? God loves that, too. Dream.

Here's a great song recommendation: "Goodness of God" by Bethel Music.

Laughter Is Good Medicine

A cheerful heart is good
medicine, but a crushed spirit
dries up the bones.
PROVERBS 17:22 (NIV)

This morning, I received a message from a dear friend. She included a hilarious video with a woman dancing around her kitchen, clanging the strainer she wore as a helmet, the pot lids fastened to her chest, and the cheese grater hanging from her belt with a wooden spoon. She was a hoot! The caption? "5 minutes after have [sic] a mental breakdown from dealing with the father of my child."

I messaged my friend back: "I had one of those days yesterday. Bring out the cheese grater!"

"I would die laughing if you did this!" she replied.

I love hearing my friend laugh, so I accepted the challenge! I gathered up my costume: a strainer for a helmet, pot lids for a breastplate, a cheese grater to hang from my belt, and a wooden spoon. Then I called out to my youngest daughter: "Hey! I need you to record a video for me!"

"Mommy, what are you doing?" she asked when she saw me.

We both laughed hysterically!

"Okay, tell me when you're recording," I said once we were set up.

"I *am* recording!"

We roared with laughter again as I danced around the kitchen clanging my lids and grater with the wooden spoon. Truly, she was mortified!

"What's so funny?" my older daughter asked as she came down the stairs, having gotten ready for school.

She saw me and started backing away.

"Wait!" I said. "Look at my video!"

I extended my phone to her, but she held up her hand. "Nope, nope! I do not want to see this!"

She turned and bolted back up the stairs.

My videographer and I howled in the kitchen.

I sent the video to my friend and then spent the rest of the day glancing at my phone, anticipating her response. I couldn't wait to hear her belly laugh!

Honestly, I get bogged down and discouraged by the onslaught of drama from my ex and his flying monkeys. There literally is no reprieve. I've experienced the all-out fatigue that comes from ongoing high conflict, but I don't want to live my days in exhaustion. I don't want to look back and feel regret over having wasted so much time and energy on him. Ugh!

We had a good dose of medicine that morning, and it carried me throughout the day. Who am I kidding? It carried me throughout the week.

ACTIVITY:

I'm not going to make you wear a strainer for a hat, strategically place the potlids and cheese grater on your body, and dance around the kitchen banging them with a wooden spoon! But I won't stop you, either.

On second thought, I do challenge you. Do it! Take that video and send it to your Square Squad, or at least one person in your Square Squad. They know your journey and will rejoice with you in your cheerful heart! Play today. Laugh a good old belly laugh.

Who Is the Head?

> Wives, subject yourselves to
> your own husbands, as to the
> Lord. For the husband is the
> head of the wife, as Christ also
> is the head of the church, He
> Himself being the Savior of
> the body. But as the church
> is subject to Christ, so also
> the wives ought to be to their
> husbands in everything.
> **EPHESIANS 5:22-24 (NASB)**

I'm going to be honest here. The NASB translation of this verse has never sat well with me. It raises a few questions. Is a husband equal with Christ? Does a husband take the place of God in a marriage? Does a husband save his wife? Do I have to obey my husband? Do I have to obey him when he is clearly sinning?

None of this makes sense to me.

In Bible college, we were taught about the dangers of building a doctrine on a few verses. We discussed the phrase "let scripture interpret scripture." We already know that a person can't be equal with Christ (Philippians 2:6–8). We also know that salvation comes through Jesus's death and resurrection (Romans 1:3–4, 1 Corinthians 15:3–4). We must obey God rather than man (Acts 5:29). Further, Paul teaches that there is mutuality in marriage (1

Corinthians 7:3–4). We also know that biblical leadership isn't about craving and abusing power (Matthew 20:26–28).

The typical teaching of headship and submission—that a husband has the final say in all things and a wife obeys without question—does not jive with the rest of scripture.

Further, numerous women in the Bible served the Lord as strong and respected leaders in their churches, communities, and nations. Moreover, several respectable and godly wives in the Bible were praised and were certainly not required to ask their husband for permission before making a decision. We know that the Proverbs 31 woman didn't ask her husband for permission in her business dealings, and he didn't micromanage her (Proverbs 31). Abigail didn't submit to her foolish husband, and she saved her whole household (1 Samuel 25). Priscilla's name is always mentioned before her husband's name. This was significant in their day because it signified Priscilla's place of honour in the church.

These women were respected in their own right and submission isn't even part of the accounts. Ladies, we get to be full-fledged adults!

Another important theological practice I learned in Bible college is to pay attention to a passage's larger context. Ephesians 5 is about unity and Christ's love for the church. The hunger for hierarchy is in direct opposition to that message. Why would a biblical teaching on love, unity, and servant leadership suddenly shift into a power dynamic in marriage? Simply put, it doesn't. Selfish hierarchy has no place in the body of Christ, let alone in marriage. If someone's doctrine allows it, there's something wrong with that doctrine and it must be examined.

Today's devotional barely touches the surface of this hot topic! Many people have conducted extensive research into this. Bruce C.E. Fleming and his wife Joy Flemming are both scholars and have written books on this topic. Cynthia Long Westfall wrote a book called *Paul and Gender*. Gretchen Baskerville has written extensively on the topic. Author Sheila Wray Gregoire notes that marriages work better when a husband and wife make decisions together. Leslie Vernick has also written articles on headship and submission.

If you're interested in this topic, be sure to seek out these writings, as well as other scholars and teachers in the field.

ACTIVITY:
Reflect on these questions in your journal. What have you been taught about headship and submission? Is what you've been taught consistent with scripture? Has headship and submission brought about love and unity to your marriage, or has it brought you pain, destruction, and misery? If the NASB translation doesn't sit well with you, research! Arm yourself with knowledge.

View Ourselves Rightly

Don't think you are better than
you really are. Be honest in
your evaluation of yourselves,
measuring yourselves by the
faith God has given us.

ROMANS 12:3 (NLT)

Ever since a dear friend pointed this verse out to me, it has been so helpful. It cautions us against pride. Honest self-reflection helps us to see our strengths and weaknesses. We measure ourselves by God's standard.

I was constantly beaten down emotionally, psychologically, and spiritually in my marriage. According to my ex, I was deficient in every way. It was common for him to badger me as he followed me around the house. I would make my way to the bedroom or bathroom and lock the door, but he would take the door off its hinges so he could finish his tirade.

On one such occasion, he was clarifying for me which one of us was the most spiritual (spoiler alert: it wasn't me).

"Jane, you don't even have the fruit of the Spirit!" he said. "Where is your kindness? Goodness? Look at me! I'm overflowing with the fruit of the Spirit! I bring people to church. I tithe. I'm generous and people know it! What do you do? Nothing!"

That's quite the demonstration of the fruit of the Spirit! It's almost laughable now, but at the time I had to work hard to counter these onslaughts. I became a shell of myself.

In a healthy relationship, I imagine that a husband would give his wife helpful feedback, and vice versa, like *"iron sharpens iron"* (Proverbs 27:17, NIV). There was a time when I would consider his words and wonder whether I was acting the way he said I was. But he and his flying monkeys have long since lost the right to speak into my life.

I must view myself rightly and remind myself of who God says I am. I have strengths and weakness for sure, and I'm open to hearing about them from God, respected mentors, and my Square Squad.

I've been blasted with many lies about who I am from my ex and his flying monkeys. Recently, he was planning a trip with one of our daughters and I had some scheduling concerns. Wanting his way, he attacked my character.

"How can you be so selfish?" he demanded. "Why aren't you putting our daughter first?"

This was part of his manipulation tactic. He knows I don't want to be selfish, and he knows our children matter to me. I was, in fact, putting our daughter's needs first.

His tactics have less power over me now because I care less about what others think of me. I see his comments for what they are: foolish manipulation.

Even still, I need to counter these lies with the truth. And so I use "AND" language. I learned this tool from a conference I attended.

State the lie and then counter it with five truths.

The lie: he says that I'm selfish and don't care about our daughter's needs, implying that I'm not a good mother. The truth: I'm a great mother!

I counter this by saying to myself (not him!):

I am putting our daughter first, by considering her school schedule.
AND
I am cultivating a strong relationship with my daughter.
AND
When I see that our daughter needs something, like counselling, and he blocks it, I take the matter to court. Then the judge puts it in a court order. I am reasonable and the judge thinks so, too!
AND
I see my daughter's talents and interests and provide opportunities for her to grow, learn, and enjoy life.
AND
I teach my daughter about the things of God.

ACTIVITY:

What are some lies you've been told? Give this "AND" language a try and be honest in your evaluation of yourself. You have many strengths, so go ahead and name them! It's not prideful; it's viewing yourself rightly.

We are fully known and loved by God.

For a song to go along with this devotional, I recommend "Known" by Tauren Wells.

Are We Supposed to Be Doormats?

> Then Peter came to Jesus and
> asked, "Lord, how many times
> shall I forgive my brother or
> sister who sins against me? Up
> to seven times?"
> Jesus answered, "I tell you,
> not seven times, but seventy-
> seven times."
>
> **MATTHEW 18:21–22 (NIV)**

I was taught that this passage teaches unconditional forgive-ness—in other words, limitless forgiveness in every situation. The message I got from certain family members, church members, and well-meaning counsellors was clear: it was irrelevant how many times he sinned against me; my job was to forgive and stay married, no exceptions.

Family members sent me scriptures about how I needed to forgive. They told me that since my ex and I weren't reconciled, I was harbouring unforgiveness. For them, it was simple: forgive his sin. The next time he did the same thing, I was just supposed to forgive him again and again and again. Their reasoning was that God gives us multiple second chances, so we should do likewise.

But it isn't that simple. Was I supposed to forgive him every time he watched porn when he just kept feeding his desires without making any attempt to stop? Was I supposed to forgive him every time he gave me the silent treatment for days on end, which only ever ended when he had to leave on a business trip and wanted some affection before he took off? Was I supposed to forgive him and turn a blind eye for lying as naturally as breathing? Was I supposed to forgive him for cheating and then lying to cover it up? Was I supposed to forgive him when he hurt our children over and over? Was I supposed to just forgive and pretend everything was fine?

Is that Jesus's message? No, it isn't.

Forgiveness is essential in repairing relationships, and that's what makes the misuse of this passage so sneaky.

For relationships to last, forgiveness and contrition are both important. Let's look at Luke 17:3–4:

> If your brother or sister sins against you, rebuke them;
> and if they repent, forgive them. Even if they sin against
> you seven times in a day and seven times come back to
> you saying "I repent," you must forgive them. (NIV)

Does the destructive man in your life repent? Sometimes they can offer fake apologies, like "I'm sorry you feel that way" or "I'm sorry you misheard me." When my ex and I separated, he made the rounds to family members and friends apologizing for the tip-of-the-iceberg mistakes he had made in our relationship. But he didn't apologize to me for anything. This is a manipulative tactic, not true repentance.

True repentance requires the guilty party to fully acknowledge his wrongdoing, accept responsibility, and make amends to the people he wronged. Look at Isaiah 55:7: *"Let the wicked forsake their ways and the unrighteous their thoughts. Let them turn to the Lord, and he will have mercy on them, and to our God, for he will freely pardon"* (NIV). God will abundantly pardon the guilty one who repents. Forgiveness does not excuse, permit, or ignore bad behaviour.

What happens when we keep sinning after learning the truth? What happened when Israel kept sinning against God? God divorced Israel (Jeremiah 3:8). It's impossible to have a healthy relationship with someone who keeps on sinning, period. It's possible to forgive and still separate and even divorce.

Can we forgive without contrition? Absolutely! We can and we should, but keep in mind that forgiveness alone will not repair the relationship. Forgiveness can pave the way for reconciliation, but it's only part of the equation.

In today's passage, it sounds like Peter may have been looking for a reason to stop forgiving. Let that not be us.

Forgiveness is essential for my well-being because it releases me from my ex's sinful actions and allows me to live my life to the fullest. Forgiveness is a process to allow me to work through my resentment. It's not a process whereby I ignore his ongoing, purposeful sin and pretend there are no consequences for it.

ACTIVITY:
How has the destructive man in your life hurt you? How does it make you feel? What are the consequences you've suffered because of his sin?

Using this chart as a guide, write down in your journal the offence, the feelings it left you with, and the consequences you suffered because of his sin.

Offence	Your Feelings	Consequences you suffered because of his sin

Here is a list of feelings you may want to use:

Alone	Frazzled	Nervous	Shame
Ashamed	Grief	Numb	Stressed
Betrayed	Heartbroken	Overwhelmed	Suspicious
Confused	Helpless	Paralyzed	Threatened
Depleted	Hopeless	Rattled	Trapped
Disappointed	Hurt	Rejected	Uneasy
Dismissed	Infuriated	Resentful	Unloved
Disturbed	Irritated	Sad	Vulnerable
Embarrassed	Lonely	Scared	Worried
Foolish	Mistreated	Shaken	Worthless

Once you've completed your chart, pray a prayer of forgiveness for each offence. Imagine yourself at the foot of the cross with Jesus and the destructive man in your life. Then read the following script while entering your own details.

Note: this information isn't to be shared with the destructive man in your life because the process is between you and God. If he brings up an offence he committed against you, and he's truly repentant, he can start the discussion.

(<u>Man's name</u>), I want to talk to you about an offence. The offence is (<u>name the offence</u>). It left me feeling (<u>name the emotions</u>). I suffered many consequences because of your actions: (<u>name the consequences</u>). Because Christ has forgiven me, I forgive you and release you from the debt you owe me.

If your abuser is anything like mine, he'll keep on sinning with no regard to how it affects you or your children. What are some ways in which you can emotionally, physically, and spiritually protect yourself and your children?

What About Mercy?

He has shown you, O mortal,
what is good. And what does
the Lord require of you? To act
justly and to love mercy and to
walk humbly with your God.

MICAH 6:8 (NIV)

In this passage, God reprimanded the Israelites. He had done so much for them, but they weren't thankful. They thought they could show appreciation by offering sacrifices, but sacrifices are meaningless to the Lord when they're not accompanied by a change of heart. He wanted them to show through their lifestyle that their hearts had changed. How? They were to act justly, love mercy, and walk humbly with Him.

What is justice? Merriam Webster defines it as "being just, impartial, or fair."[20] This includes the principle of right actions and dealing with others fairly. It also relates to righteousness.

This verse calls us to act with fairness and to live in accordance with divine or moral law. We are to be fair and just in our business dealings (Psalm 112:5). We are to speak the truth (Leviticus 19:11). We are directed to seek justice for and protect the vulnerable, especially when they can't speak up for themselves (Proverbs 31:8–9). We're also told to take no part in ugly deeds of darkness, but to expose them (Ephesians 5:11). We are not to grow tired

---

[20] "Justice," *Merriam-Webster*. Date of access: August 14, 2024 (https://www.merriam-webster.com/dictionary/justice).

of doing good (Galatians 6:9–10). Exposing and fighting against injustice can be a long and difficult process. The Lord requires His followers to act justly.

What does it mean to love mercy? I often wondered how I could seek justice and be merciful at the same time because the two seemed contradictory. I often heard that no one's perfect and all marriages are hard. Was I just supposed to let it all go? I was also told that I needed to extend mercy because my ex had endured a rough childhood. After all, Jesus extends mercy to us; as a wife, I was to do the same for my husband.

Does extending mercy mean repeatedly turning a blind eye to sin? Is that what Jesus did? Does being merciful mean that there are no consequences for sin? No, it doesn't.

What is mercy? Merriam-Webster defines one part of mercy as showing compassion or forbearance for an offender.[21] God offers this kind of mercy to repentant sinners. We are sinners and deserve death and punishment, but Jesus took that upon Himself. Those who believe they are sinners, repent and turn to Jesus receive mercy. As Proverbs 28:13 says, *"Whoever conceals their sins does not prosper, but the one who confesses and renounces them finds mercy"* (NIV). Jesus paid the price so we don't have to. This is the greatest act of mercy.

It also reminds me of the parable of the unmerciful servant from Matthew 18. While settling his accounts, a king called in a man who owed him a significant amount of money. The man couldn't pay it back, so he begged the king for mercy and the king

---

[21] "Mercy," *Meriam-Webster*. Date of access: August 14, 2024 (https://www.merriam-webster.com/dictionary/mercy).

forgave his debt. This very same man wanted to collect a much smaller debt from a fellow servant who also begged for mercy, but the man threw his fellow servant in jail because he couldn't pay. When the king heard about this, he was furious and threw the man in jail until he could pay off his debt.

The moral of the story is that we should forgive and show mercy because that's how God treats us.

But mercy can be distorted. Compassion and forbearance are necessary for lasting relationships, but compassion and forbearance alone cannot sustain a relationship. This misunderstanding of mercy leads to the expectation that a wife can sustain a marriage, and even salvage it, by extending mercy to her offending husband even though he's unrepentant. She ignores the sin and he's free to live as he pleases.

Paul speaks to this dysfunctional dynamic in Romans 6:1–2: *"Shall we go on sinning so that grace may increase? By no means!"* (NIV) God doesn't use mercy to let an unrepentant guilty person keep on sinning.

Further, many people in my life were quick to point out that I needed to extend mercy, but they never held my ex to the same standard. This encouraged him to continue functioning as the unmerciful servant. Just as the unmerciful servant in the parable, my ex happily received mercy but was unwilling to extend it. Sadly, his behaviour was supported by well-meaning Christians.

A different definition of mercy relates to treating those in distress with compassion.[22] Jesus wants us to help those who are less fortunate, such as orphans and widows. Further, in the parable of

[22] Ibid.

the good Samaritan, the Samaritan cared for and provided for a man from a foreign country until he was well.

There's no doubt about it! We should extend compassion to those who need help.

That said, we are also given an admonition for each person to *"carry their own load"* (Galatians 6:5, NIV). The good Samaritan helped the wounded man until he was well and able to care for himself.

As Christians, we want to be generous and help those in need. This is what it means to love mercy.

What about walking humbly with our God? We recognize our humanity and God's sovereignty. We know that we're not perfect and don't have all the answers, but we entrust ourselves to Him. He will guide us upon the best path for our lives.

Just like the Israelites, we need to show by the way we live that our hearts have changed. We are to love justice, love mercy, and walk humbly with our God. If the destructive men in our lives claim to be Christians, they should govern themselves by the same standards. A destructive man doesn't need to be absolved; he needs to be held accountable.

ACTIVITY:

What do you believe about mercy? Is it merciful to allow our husbands to keep on sinning? Is it just? How do mercy and justice coexist? Do our husbands expect mercy without extending it or cleaning up their lives? Write down your thoughts in your journal.

Don't Underestimate God

Never doubt God's mighty
power to work in you and
accomplish all this. He will
achieve infinitely more than
your greatest request, your most
unbelievable dream, and exceed
your wildest imagination! He
will outdo them all, for his
miraculous power constantly
energizes you.

EPHESIANS 3:20 (TPT)

This morning when I got out of bed, I believe God said, *"Don't underestimate Me."* Then this verse came to mind. I needed to hear it, and my guess is that it's empowering and energizing to you, too!

Ladies, we have hope. We have a reason to get out of bed in the morning. We have the most fantastic lives to live!

ACTIVITY:

What is your wildest dream? How will you honour God with the life He has given you? What beautiful dream would you regret not pursuing before you die?

During a conversation with my life coach, he asked me, "Could you live the rest of your life without doing it?" If your answer is no, then what's stopping you?

www.ingramcontent.com/pod-product-compliance
Lightning Source LLC
Chambersburg PA
CBHW060022050426
42448CB00012B/2848